Grata P9-AQB-941

PRAYER AND WORSHIP

DOUGLAS V. STEERE

ASSOCIATE PROFESSOR OF PHILOSOPHY
IN HAVERFORD COLLEGE

Fifth Printing

Price 50 cents

HAZEN BOOKS ON RELIGION
The Edward W. Hazen Foundation, Inc.

Distributed by
ASSOCIATION PRESS
347 Madison Avenue
NEW YORK

A Note about
The Hazen Books on Religion

THE purpose of this series is to present simply, compactly and inexpensively a number of the best available interpretations of the Christian philosophy as a guide to Christian living today.

The series is sponsored by the Edward W. Hazen Foundation. The responsibility for selecting the titles and authors and for planning the manufacture and distribution of the volumes rests with the following committee: John C. Bennett (chairman), Wilbur Davies, Georgia Harkness, S. M. Keeny, Benson Y. Landis, Mrs. W. W. Rockwell, William L. Savage, George Stewart, Henry P. Van Dusen, and a representative of the Edward W. Hazen Foundation. The responsibility for the subject matter of the volumes rests with the authors alone.

The following twelve volumes comprise the series:

Christianity—and Our World. By John C. Bennett. (Nine printings)

Jesus. By Mary Ely Lyman. (Seven printings)

God. By Walter Horton. (Five printings)

Religious Living. By Georgia Harkness. (Eight printings)

Toward a World Christian Fellowship. By Kenneth Scott Latourette. (Three printings)

Prayer and Worship. By Douglas Steere. (Five printings)

The Church. By George Stewart. (Three printings)

Christians in an Unchristian Society. By Ernest Fremont Tittle. (Three printings)

What Is Man? By Robert L. Calhoun. (Three printings)

Christian Faith and Democracy. By Gregory Vlastos. (Four printings)

The Bible. By Walter Russell Bowie. (Three printings)

Reality and Religion. By Henry P. Van Dusen. (Two printings)

The publication of these books is a co-operative, non-profit enterprise for everybody concerned.

TO THE MOST GENEROUS OF FRIENDS AND COLLEAGUES

RUFUS M. JONES

WHO FOR A LONG GENERATION HAS QUICKENED IN MEN
A SENSE OF THE NEARNESS OF GOD

CONTENTS

CHAPTER I

INTRODUCTION

"Blessed are those drowsy ones for they shall soon nod to sleep."—
Nietzsche

In a conversation that I had recently with Alf Ahlberg, the head of a workers' folk-high school in central Sweden, he told me of a recent visit with a young worker who was hostile to Christianity. He asked the young man whether he disagreed with Christians because they worked for peace and justice in the world. "No!" He asked him if he was opposed to Christians preaching neighbor-love in the world. "No!" There was a pause, and then the young man continued, "I guess that what I resent in Christians is not that they are Christians, but that they are not Christian enough!"

Unless I am mistaken, the ruthless honesty of Christian youth today would lead them to accept this word of diagnosis "not Christian enough" as well deserved. For they are not blind to the "nothing in excess" attitude in contemporary liberal Christianity. Nor are they unaware of the fear that most Christians would experience if they actually received the very power for which they have prayed.

Jesus and his friends tramping the roads of Galilee; Bernard of Clairvaux and his twenty-nine companions knocking at the door of the despairing reformed Benedictine congregation at Citeaux ready to enter and sustain it; Francis of Assisi and his devoted handful of daring confreres rebuilding San Damiano and discovering that security of fellowship that replaces security of possessions; the loyal lay-friends of Gerard Groote and Florentius Radewyn living together, supporting themselves by copying manuscripts,

1

and offering hostel and religious instruction to the poor
youth of Deventer in Holland; Ignatius Loyola, Francis
Xavier, and their number conspiring together to found
the Society of Jesus and to go to the ends of the earth to
open up new fields of conquest for the church; George Fox
and his early company in Lancashire proclaiming the need
not for words but for life here and now in the new order;
Newman, Pusey, Froude, and their friends at Oxford restoring the organic sense of the Christian Society; Kagawa and
his New Life societies in Japan; Grenfell and his socio-
medical work in Labrador; Schweitzer and his medical-
mission to Central Africa—these are all Christian associations that a man who took the Christian way seriously could
join. These are authentic. They are evidences of men laid
hold of by a devotion that has made life, and a particular
way of life, intensely important. If the Christian Church
could multiply their kind, what power on earth could
resist it?

The power is there. How may it be laid hold upon?
How can Christians remain content with the apparently
incurable mediocrity of soul that fills the Christian ranks?

Here is the problem of this book: How does a man become increasingly a Christian when he already is one? How
does he begin from where he is and at least be in motion
away from "not Christian enough"? In other words, this
book is concerned with growth in the religious life.

A look at the life of any one of these practising Christians who have just been mentioned will show that what
distinguishes them from most Christians is not the cataclys-
mic circumstances of their entry into the religious life, but
the fact that over a period of years they grew out of what they
were into what we know them to have become. For each
of these men—both at and after his conscious entry into the
religious life, whether that entry was very dramatic or very

simple—was entering upon the long-pull, upon a *life*. And upon that entry he was at a very different stage of growth from that in which we find him at maturity. At the end of his life, Francis of Assisi could gather his beloved followers and entreat them, "Let us begin, Brethren, to serve our Lord God, for until now we have made but little progress." But the humble brother Francis who made that request was a different Francis from the proud young merchant-poet who knelt before the crucifix at San Damiano some twenty years before. Why does Francis grow and deepen steadily from the time of his entry into the religious life until his death, and why do most Christians atrophy away on the early plateaus of the religious life? This is a central problem in the religious life, which the almost exclusive focus of attention upon the original initiation into the life itself, upon "conversion," has almost completely neglected.

It is of no use to look at these great men and women as a kind of a spiritual luxury and to be sure that ordinary men and women must not be asked to share in such growth. We have been insulated from them for too long by regarding these men and women as saints set apart from us by the comfortable gulf of belief that they possess some special bent for sanctity that is not for us. This gulf is one of our own making. For the only difference between the stunted irresoluteness, distraction, half-thoughts, half-resolutions, indecisiveness, and great moments with which most of us occupy our time and the quiet strength of these we have set apart as saints (as Evelyn Underhill in her *Mixed Pastures* so truly says) "is not the possession of abnormal faculties but the completeness of their abandonment to the over-ruling spirit and the consequent transformation of personality."

This book is concerned with the practices that assist this transformation. It attempts no justification for the Christian life.[1] It proposes no intellectual world-view in which the relation between the demands of this inner life and the rest of experience is developed.[2] It presupposes the experience of having felt and faced at some time the claim of this life. It is concerned with the growth and cultivation of the religious life, which, for it, means growth in *devotion*. The modern mind does not like this word *devotion*. It often does not understand it. Devotion is steady. Listen to one of the spiritual counsellors of the late eighteenth century: "We are not devout," wrote Jean Grou, "just because we are able to reason well about the things of God, nor because we have grand ideas or fine imaginations about spiritual matters, nor because we are sometimes affected by tears. Devotion is not a thing which passes, which comes and goes, as it were, but it is something habitual, fixed, permanent, which extends over every instant of life and regulates all our conduct." And devotion is swift and gay: No one has ever surpassed the distinguished spiritual guide of the early seventeenth century, Francis de Sales, at this point: "Devotion, is simply the promptitude, fervour, affection, and agility which we have in the service of God: and there is a difference between a good man and a devout man; for he is a good man who keeps the commandments of God, although it be without great promptitude or fervour; but he is devout who not only observes them but does so willingly, promptly, and with a good heart."

The life of devotion will grow in this steadiness and in this agility. Those who possess it are often plain people. They often bear scars. They may have been at one time very difficult personalities. There is a striking realism in their recognition of the power of the destructive forces that dissipate and divide life, of the cleft between the ideal and

---

[1] See John Bennett, *Christianity—and Our World* (Association Press).
[2] See Walter Horton, *God* (Association Press).

the real. Yet they seem to see beneath the cleft, to be confi-
dent that it can be healed, and to turn up at unexpected
moments, prepared for action. For them marriage, and
birth, and the family, and the community, and work, and
the seasons, and even suffering and death are good—for they,
too, are related to the center. These men and women seem
to be living from within outwards and to be inwardly awake
and alive. They are far from perfect in their conduct, but
they usually know where they are weak and they are not led
to conceal it from themselves or to be unnerved by it. They
are teachable. And they seem to be extremely well satisfied with their schoolmaster.

The saints and these plain people understand one another
remarkably well, and these plain devout Christians are at
home with the counsel of the saints. The saint may not be
the best theologian, as some have claimed, but he is not to
be scorned if what we are seeking is to know the nature of
the self, of its errors, of its evasions, of its cultivation; in
short, if we are seeking out a much-needed psychology of
the deeper reaches of life. It is significant that psycholo-
gists such as C. G. Jung and Fritz Künkel have recognized
a deeper rôle for psychotherapy than it has hitherto acknowledged. Where it has been content until recently to
devote itself to the salvaging of the mentally sick, it is now
beginning to sense a deeper function: that of assisting those
who already possess a mediocre adjustment but who are
sick unto life and are reaching out for more creative levels,
levels of greater abandonment, of more effective freedom.
In approaching this field they are at once faced with the
spiritual problem. And they, too, are at once driven back
to these pioneers of the spiritual life. They scarcely need
the strong words of a philosopher like A. E. Taylor, who
emphasizes the costliness of any worth-while discoveries in
this field:

"The psychologist who can teach us anything of the realities of the moral or religious life is not the Professor who satisfies a mere intellectual curiosity by laboratory experiments, or the circulation of *questionnaires* about the dates and circumstances of other men's 'conversions,' or 'mystical experiences.' A man might spend a long life at that business without making himself or his readers a whit the wiser. So long as he looks on at the type of experience he is investigating simply from the outside, he can hope to contribute nothing to its interpretation. He is in the position of a congenitally blind or deaf man attempting to construct a theory of beauty, in nature or art, by 'circularising' his seeing and hearing friends with questions about their favourite color-schemes or combinations of tones. The psychological records really relevant for our purpose are first and foremost those of the men who have actually combined the experience of the saint, or the aspirant after sanctity, with the psychologist's gift of analysis, the Augustines and Pascals, and next those of the men who have had the experiences, even when they have been unable to analyse and criticise them, the Susos and the Bunyans. Mere analytical and critical acumen without a relevant experience behind it should count for nothing, since in this, as in all matters which have to do with the interpretation of personal life, we can only read the soul of another by the light of that which we know 'at first hand' within ourselves."[3]

It is nothing new to these psychotherapists to know that the cost of inner discoveries and of inner cultivation is high. They are ready to go to school to these devotional masters and learn their way. They are prepared to give to the exploration of the inner life of man a precision, a care, and a discipline comparable in its own manner to that which

---

[3] *Faith of a Moralist* I, 17-18 (Macmillan).

has been devoted to the investigation of the physical world. They know from many years of practice that it requires the most regular discipline to develop a really adequate response to another level of life than that in which a man has been accustomed to functioning. They never conceal it from him.

It is in this same spirit that this little book must constantly consult the articulate saints and quote freely from them. When a man is unconscious and you are working over him with artificial respiration, you often have to make the lungs move many times before he begins to take over the function for himself, and the early breaths on his own initiative have to be meticulously watched lest he relapse again. Without practice, without discipline, without continuous devotion, without failure, correction, re-dedication, re-orientation, the writer knows of no growth in the religious life—which to him is not an episode, or an event, but a *life*.

What is set forth here will naturally find readers at different stages of growth. Therefore, what may be useful to one may mean nothing to another. It seeks only to suggest, not to prescribe. Phillips Brooks used to tell his friends that when a fish was served to them, it was not necessary either to reject it because it contained bones or to eat it bones and all. A wise diner calmly and patiently separated the flesh he wished to eat from the bones, enjoyed it, and went away content. There could be no wiser suggestion for the use of a book on religious practice.

This book will rejoice when it finds the reader who is able to say either on a first or a subsequent reading that such suggestions are now superfluous to him, that he has found his own way. Now, like Lancelot Andrewes (1555-1626), he is ready perhaps to write his own manual of devotional practice. This he will go on revising and recasting, as Andrewes did, until he leaves this life. For any forms of the cultivation of the religious life are in themselves always subject to change in order to meet the changing needs of the seeker. They are scaffolding to be torn down and re-erected in new forms in accordance with the stage of growth of the life structure they seek to aid. To take them as an end in themselves is idolatry and blasphemy.

Yet the temporary character of any specific practices that seek to encourage or to give expression to the religious life need in no way blind us to their importance. Instruction in painting and in music is perhaps only a passing stage in the development of the innate genius of a great master. But none of them ever reached the stage where it was superfluous without it. Perhaps no area has been so neglected in our generation as adult religious practice. I can put my hand on a dozen expertly written books on the theological controversies of the day that deal with the defense of religion against its secular attackers. But outside the works of Evelyn Underhill, my shelves seem to carry but few recent books by living writers[4] that are of equal caliber and freshness and insight that give me help in the cultivation and nurture of the religious life itself. There have been glimpses here and there, but this field is left principally to the compilers of devotional anthologies, or to those who retouch, re-frame, re-illustrate conventional counsel without re-thinking it in the light of existing needs; or to those who would parasitically exploit religion of its social and therapeutic qualities with only the most shallow conception of what is meant by the *demands* of religion, by what Albertus Magnus called "adhering to God."

To sum up: the real enemy of the Christian fellowship is itself. It is the low level of mediocrity of devotion with

---

[4] Georgia Harkness, *Religious Living* (Association Press); Hornell Hart, *Living Religion* (Abingdon); Wieman's *Methods of Private Religious Living* (Macmillan) are a few exceptions to be noted.

which the majority of Christians are content. The Christian fellowship is "not Christian enough."

Søren Kierkegaard, the Danish Pascal, once told a story: One time there was a wild duck used to the freedom of the trackless wilderness of the air. On one of his migrations north he chanced to alight in a farm-yard where the tame ducks were being fed. He ate some of their corn and liked it so much that he lingered until the next meal, and then the next week, and month, until the autumn came and his old companions flew over the farm-yard and gave their cry to him that it was time to be away. The old ecstasy roused within him again and he flapped his wings in order to join them, but he could not leave the ground. He had grown fat on the farmer's corn and the indolent life of the barnyard. He resigned himself to remain there, and each season until his death the calls of his fellows roused him— but each year the calls seemed fainter and further away. The wild duck had become a tame duck.

The quickening of this good man, this tame man into the fervent and devout man, is the task of devotion. Three aids are set forth here: private prayer, corporate worship, and devotional reading.

CHAPTER II

THE PRACTICE OF PRIVATE PRAYER: I

"There is that near you which will guide you; O wait for it, and be sure ye keep it."—Isaac Penington

THE NATURE OF PRAYER

"Ostriches never fly; fowls fly, but heavily, low down, and seldom; but eagles, doves, and swallows fly often, swiftly, and on high." Once more Francis de Sales is contrasting the drowsy ones, the "good" ones, and the devout ones. Of all the practices that serve to arouse this spiritual nimbleness and swiftness and vivacity of devotion, none is so central as the practice of private prayer. In fact, this practice is in itself an act of devotion. For the great Christian men and women of prayer have always looked upon prayer as a *response* to the ceaseless outpouring love and concern with which God lays siege to every soul.

Prayer for them is a response to the prior love of God. Nearly a thousand years ago Bernard of Clairvaux gave a matchless word on this in a talk to his religious brotherhood: "Do you awake? Well, He too is awake. If you rise in the nighttime, if you anticipate to your utmost your earliest awaking, you will already find Him waking—you will never anticipate His own awakeness. In such an intercourse you will always be rash if you attribute any priority and predominant share to yourself; for He loves both more than you, and before you love at all."

The prayer of devotion is a response, a reply, the only appropriate reply that a man or a woman could make who had been made aware of the love at the heart of things, the love that environed them, that rallied them, that wearied out evil and indifference by its patient joy. To sense that is for a man to long to love back through every relationship that he touches. "I trow God offers himself to me as he does to the highest angel," Meister Eckhart, the great German mystic, cries out, "and were I as apt as he is, I should receive as he does." And in one of his later sermons Meister Eckhart went a step further and could say, of God's own delight in this outpouring of His love, "The joy and satisfaction of it are ineffable. It is like a horse turned loose in a lush meadow giving vent to his horse nature by galloping full tilt about the field; he enjoys it and it is his nature. And just in the same way God's joy and satisfaction in his likes finds vent in his pouring out his entire nature and his being into this likeness." With such a consciousness of the love of God, is it any wonder that in Eckhart's day, in the fourteenth century, we hear of an old woman who was seen coming along the streets of Strasbourg carrying a pail of water in one hand and a torch in the other? When asked what she was about, she answered that with the pail of water she was going to put out the flames of hell and with the torch she was going to burn up heaven, so that in the future men could love the dear Lord God for himself alone and not out of fear of hell or out of craving for reward.

Prayer then is simply a form of waking up out of the dull sleep in which our life has been spent in half-intentions, half-resolutions, half-creations, half-loyalties, and a becoming actively aware of the real character of that which we are and of that which we are over against. It is an opening of drowsy lids. It is a shaking off of grave-clothes. It is a dip into acid. It is a daring to "read the text of the universe in the original." "We should in ourselves learn and perceive who we are, how and what our life is, what God is and is doing in us, what he will have from us, and to what ends he will or will not use us," says John Tauler, a disciple of Eckhart's.

To know and to love God directly is to come to know what we are. All true Christian prayer also presupposes the further step, that there are things He will have from us and that some of our responses are true and authentic responses to His love and others are not. Prayer is an attempt to get ourselves into that active co-operation with God where we may discern what is authentic and be made ready to carry it out.

With our increased knowledge about the continuous re-organization of life that goes on in the depths of the unconscious, the impressive definition of prayer as *the soul's sincere desire* has appeared. In this sense the fearful man prays by his acts of withdrawal, of cringing, of brooding, of distrust; and the man of faith prays by his openness, freedom, readiness to take risks, trust of the future. Both pray by these acts even though they are not conscious of them as prayer. There is a large measure of truth in this interpretation. For many forms of prayer do send down into the unconscious: positive imagery, positive resolutions, positive incentives to action. And these forms of prayer would willingly recognize that these elements operate within the unconscious to aid, and to bring into fruition in the life of inward desire what is begun above the threshold of consciousness, what is intentionally and consciously sought after in prayer. Yet since this deep unconscious intention of the soul is able to be reached and affected by consciously directed intention, *prayer* in this sense becomes not merely *the soul's sincere desire,* but prayer is the process of intentionally turning the focus of the soul's sincere desire upon the active nature of the Divine Love and by every device within its power holding it there until it becomes engaged.

There is no fear here of the charge of autosuggestion in prayer that so haunted the last generation. It is freely admitted from the outset that large elements of prayer are and should be of that character. One wise writer has suggested recently that the very purpose of the active cultivation of the interior life is to transform the gifts of grace into an effective autosuggestion. All that is meant by this word autosuggestion, or self-suggestion, is that the suggestion is selected and presented by the person to himself. We have come to recognize that all that we know has been suggested to us either by our external or internal environment in the form of what is called heterosuggestion.

In entering prayer we have a perfect right to choose from this random mass of heterosuggestions some that we regard as more significant than others, and to dwell upon them. "Whatsoever things are true, whatsoever things are honest, whatsoever things are just, whatsoever things are pure, whatsoever things are lovely, whatsoever things are of good report; if there be any virtue, and if there be any praise, think on these things." Autosuggestion is no more than this act of dwelling upon selected aspects of experience. By the mere act of dwelling upon them we do not necessarily prove them to be true. Nor did we intend to. That matter of truth is both a prior and a subsequent matter of tests and interpretations to which either auto- or heterosuggestions must be submitted. These selected aspects of experience with which we may enter prayer are, however, only a threshold of past experience that we cross in order to engage with what is there. And they are subject to revision and to addition as the prayer brings its bearer to new levels of insight.

Prayer is often defined as *speech with God*. It may begin that way. But prayer of a high order rarely stops there. Real prayer is more nearly *work* with God. In Japan, a student of painting is not allowed to touch his brush to the canvas until he has spent hours moving first his body and then his brush in a synchronizing response to the curves of the mountain he would paint. This empathy, this *feeling into* the subject by the body and the limbs, is not unlike prayer. The swift and agile acts of devotion that follow are only the setting down on the canvas of daily life what is felt into and moved into and yielded to in prayer.

In prayer, what looks like passivity may conceal the most intense activity. It may in truth be "a rest most busy." Unless there be that coincidence of wills, which means that the human will is brought low, is tendered, is transformed, the New Testament is quite clear that its amazing promises of the power of prayer do not apply: *"If ye abide in me, and my words abide in you,* ye shall ask what ye will and it shall be done unto you." In the most real prayer of all there is wrought that refocusing of the life of the one who prays until he is brought to abide in the Divine love and the character of the Divine love to abide in him. Then and then only does the promise of extending that transforming power indefinitely really hold. At those moments a man comes to recognize the distinction between his praying and his being prayed in, and to realize that most of what has been described above is only *praying* and that what really matters is to *be prayed in.*

To the prayer of the woman who begged that the wicked Dean Inge might die, to the prayers for the preservation of his ecclesiastical property made by an official of a church that still held its buildings although it had lost its people, to the prayers of an army chaplain that the enemy be destroyed, to the prayers of a student on the matter of his life partner, for the confirmation of an accomplished decision that he had no intention of changing—to these prayers apply the piercing ray of this prescription: *"If ye abide in me and my words abide in you,* ye shall ask. . . ." By the light of this condition, the flesh of selfish lust and desire melts away and only the firm bony structure of the true willingness to cooperate with the Divine remains. Unless you are ready and willing to seek that kind of inner empathy and submit to that kind of inner renovation, it would be better not to play at praying.

WE NEED TO BE ALONE

The first condition of the practice of private prayer is to be able to be alone. For many, this is not an easy matter. The hail of irrelevant stimuli to which our modern life seems increasingly to subject us, the often unrealized attraction that a thin form of gregariousness holds for us that keeps us either in or planning to be in the company of others during most of our waking hours, the pressure and temporarily satisfying narcotic of intense busyness in outward occupations—these all seem to make us bent on distracting rather than on gathering ourselves. If modern man is to have any growth of his inward life and understanding that will penetrate below the level of the obvious, he must meet this increase in randomness, this immersion in outward dispersion with a deliberate increase of purpose and planning to be able to be alone in order to open himself to the positive field of recollecting forces that operate there. Anker-Larsen, a well-known Danish writer, tells of an old Danish peasant who on his death bed asked of his son only one promise: that he should sit *alone* for a half-hour each day in the best room of the house. "The son did this and became a model for the whole district. This Father's command had taken thought for everything: for Eternity, soul-deepening, refinement, history." A Southern friend, Anna May Stokely, has told me of her mother, who, after her husband's death, was left with several young children and with only the management of a small peanut plantation in Virginia from which to earn the means for their support. She managed with a quiet poise and strength that was felt by all about her. With all of the duties and responsibilities that she carried, she had an inviolable custom of retiring in the middle of the morning into a little sitting room, and the children knew that only in case of urgent need was she to be disturbed. She bought, often at great price, this time for the healing of the soul. For her it was easy to admit that perhaps the great saints and other great people might encroach upon or dispense with the time for recharging, but that she in her need could not. The regularity with which Francis of Assisi found it necessary to withdraw from the brothers in order to be made fit to be among them, and the habitual practice that the New Testament suggests about Jesus' practice of retirement for prayer, when it says, "as he was wont," makes it likely that they, too, would have joined Mrs. Stokely in making an exception for the *great* saints that they were not at liberty to make for themselves.

The first condition of private prayer is to recognize that solitude is the stronghold of the strong, and to provide for its place in life. Thomas More, Henry VIII's Lord High Chancellor, charged with his heavy duties of state, made provision to take the whole of each Friday for inner healing, for retirement, and for religious reading. These men and women have found that there is a maintenance cost to the spiritual life. "Imports must balance exports." They do not boast of what they do. They are very gentle with others. But they have learned the necessity of this for themselves. Communion with God is no longer a luxury but a necessity for them. "Twelve years ago, I undertook to practice prayer in earnest," wrote Winifred Kirkland in her *As Far As I Can See,* "something very different from my previous sleepy petitions as I snuggled into bed, and also different from the terror-stricken appeals I had sent to God when some loved-one was in peril, or I myself was threatened with despair. Twelve years ago I found it hard enough to hold my attention on my praying for ten minutes a day, now an hour is not enough for the direction and the communion that have become as indispensable as my food and drink."

There is no use trying to conceal how difficult it is to find time for private prayer in the congested schedules under which most modern people live. But at bottom it is not a question of finding time, it is a question of the depth of the sense of need and of the desire. Busy lovers find time to write letters to one another, often find time for long letters, although what really matters is not the length of the letter any more than it is the length of the prayer. In this life we find the time that is necessary for what we believe to be important. God never asks of men what is impossible.

Spoken Prayer

The most common form of private prayer is spoken prayer. We pour out before God our needs, our longings, our pleas for forgiveness, our aspirations, our thanksgiving, our commendation of others. This may be in the form of some classic prayer that we have learned and that acts as the vehicle for our feelings. It may be spontaneous. My wife's grandfather used to get up early and go out to the barn long before the family were accustomed to rise, and there on his knees he would talk over his life and his family and his work and his friends before God. That was real. It was more than a lecture. As he spoke, something searched him and worked in and on him. The divine-human engagement was in process. One look at his face in that old picture of his in the hall is enough to convince you of that.

There is something firm and tangible and arresting about the prayer that is spoken aloud which holds some types of mind. Like the taking of a vow, it recommits them to their resolutions, it re-informs intention; like a spoken confession to another person, it purges them of concealed sin;

like a conversation with a friend, it brings God very near and once more it makes both His being and His way real for them. In conversation we do not address a friend as though he were a public meeting nor do we use the formal language of public address. In private spoken prayer we have the same privilege and the more we can drop the conventional phrases that may have little meaning and come to simple, sharp, clear, and direct speech, the more likely the prayer is to be genuine. To all, the discipline of spoken prayer should be at least a part of daily practices. Phrases of it will come back through the day, and if the prayer is an old friend, it may appear in you at a time of great need when all else has slipped away. And it may call you back to the center from which alone you can face creatively what is before you.

The use of the traditional kneeling posture and closed eyes in spoken prayer is an individual matter. The kneeling posture is an active bodily gesture of loving submission. I know many who find God quite as readily sitting quietly in a chair or, if they can avoid drowsiness, lying quietly in bed. I know others who speak aloud their prayers to Him while walking in secluded places. The closed eyes are a simple attempt to diminish outside stimuli that may distract. How often has the wish come that the curtains of the ears might be as readily drawn? Yet I find nothing to contradict Kagawa's assertion that scripture nowhere says we have to close our eyes when we pray. These are matters for personal experiment. Throughout the day's work or in the many intervals that come between different parts of our work we may be helped by ejaculatory prayers, "the little cries to God": a word, a verse, renews us and calls back our intention.

CHAPTER III

THE PRACTICE OF PRIVATE PRAYER: II

"In one short hour you can learn more from the inward voice than you could learn from man in a thousand years."—John Tauler

SILENT PRAYER

Few go far into prayer before they discover that the *work* that goes on in prayer may, during at least a part of the period, go on best of all in silence. And yet to get to this silence we have to cross a ditch that separates it from the rest of our lives. For we live in a talking world where loquacity is at a premium. When we sit together with others we must either be talking or listening to others talk, or to speech electrically transmitted and received through the radio. Man in our time has become what Bergson calls *Homo Loquax,* and how many have become as the early church father, Clement of Alexandria, says, like old shoes—all worn out but the tongue. Yet nearly all the great experiences of loyalty, of love, of suffering take place beyond the spoken word: Augustine's experience with his mother at Ostia; the saintly French King Louis and the Franciscan, Brother Giles, meeting, embracing, and separating in silence at Assisi; Mary, the mother of Jesus, weeping silently at the foot of the cross. In each of these scenes we are brought back to what the eighteenth-century Quaker John Woolman's old Indian friend Papunehang tenderly described when he spoke of how he loved "to feel where words come from."

Only when you can walk or ride or paddle a canoe or sit by the fire with a companion and be in most active fellowship with him without the need for conversation do you really know and trust each other. If the oven door is always

19

open, the heat escapes. There is a gathering of warmth, a revelation of the inner nature of each, and a charging of the positive bond of friendship if the silence is a living one in which you enjoy each other. Early in the friendship this is not easy. There you are likely to talk much, for you are still testing one another; you are not yet sure of one another. When a crew rows a two mile race, the first half-mile they tend to row as eight individuals in spite of all of their training. After the first level in them is worn down, the particularities go, the deep togetherness comes, and the crew settles down to real joint work where the members become almost the arms and legs of a single body. In prayer, too, there comes the point where words are no longer necessary and the joint *work* can begin.

It is beyond words and in the intention that we find the real work of prayer going on. "How rare to find a soul still enough to hear God speak," said the French spiritual counsellor, Fénelon. And yet to be silent means to have a share in that stilling. It means to weary out that stubborn, forward, commanding, selfish particularity in us in order to settle down to the deeper togetherness, the real work with the divine power. "O! wait more and more," wrote the Quaker mystic, Isaac Penington, "to know, how to keep *that* silence, which is of the power; that in every one of you, what the power would have silent, may be silent . . . wait and labor, then, to know, understand, and be guided by, the motives, leadings, drawings, teachings, quickenings, etc., of the thing itself within."

There is the body that needs to be silenced. We in the West are scornful of those who would teach us how to relax the body, how to control its breathing, how to control and rest it sufficiently, and how to control its diet. Yet one day even the Christian religion will again have to attend to this training of the body. For Christianity is an incarnated religion which believes in the unity of creation, it believes that spirit indwells flesh and that each influences the other. Only by bringing the body under such vital control may we begin to silence it, "to wear it like a loose garment" in prayer. In a rudimentary way each of us can learn to rest and relax and offer up his body as the opening act of silent prayer—and to discover that certain conditions of food, sleep, exercise, development of bodily skills greatly facilitate such controlled co-operation of the body in prayer.

There are the inevitable outer distractions to silent prayer. A mother is calling her child, the wind howls against the house, the rain beats down, and at once the draw-bridge of the mind is let down and the attention rushes out across it. This is natural. There is no cause for alarm or dismay. Bring it gently back and go on. It often helps to pray the distraction directly into the prayer: "Oh God, continue to call me as the Mother does her child and I shall answer"; "the wind of God is always blowing, but I must hoist my sail"; "Oh God, saturate my soul with the rain of thy redeeming love."

Within our own minds there are also the tones of con-flicting desires, demands, problems, suggestions, and plans that even in the silence go on ringing in our ears. These must and can be ordered and quieted. To this end it is good to remember into whose presence we come in the silence. "Begin all your prayers, be they mental or vocal, with the presence of God, and make no exception to this rule," counsels Francis de Sales. "I set the Lord always in my sight," says the Psalmist.

There has recently come a growing realization that Protestantism both in its instruction for prayer and in its public worship has directed itself almost exclusively to the ear, to the neglect of the eye. This has starved those persons who take in and who preserve experience most easily in the

form of pictures. To these persons certain pictures thrown
on the screen of the mind as they begin prayer may be in-
valuable aids in helping them to center their minds and to
enter into the presence of God in prayer. Scenes from the
New Testament are commonly used. The person sees himself with Jesus at the wedding feast of Cana; or as one of the
companions, being overtaken by Jesus on the road to Em-
maus, and pictures the experience of walking and talking
and sitting down to supper with him; or as Simon the Cyrene
toiling up the hill under the weight of the cross; or kneeling with the little company at the foot of the cross.[1] Others
have turned to nature or to friendship, a still pool in a deep
wood, a grove of trees that seem like the earth's arms out-
stretched toward the sky, a freshly plowed field, the face of
a departed one who had revealed the love of God to them.
These have been patterns that some have found to be good
gateways that shut out distractions, centered the mind, and
led on into the deeper ranges of prayer where they were
left behind.

As one moves beyond these picture seeds that may have
been used to help the mind to still and gather itself in silent
prayer, one comes into the presence of the silent one. To
meet a silent one under any circumstances is to feel the power
of silence. Who has not been talkative in a group where
there is a silent one who listens, who understands all, and
who fathoms the matter at hand? In a conversation in this

---

[1] The New York woman who writes under the name of Anne Byrd
Payson in *I Follow the Road* (Abingdon) has carried this ancient
practice further and suggested the value that she and her friends have
found in choosing patterns for meditation that have a special bearing
on some weakness in their own lives that they wish to face in prayer.
To one suffering from fastidiousness, the scene of Jesus girded with the
towel washing the disciples' feet; to an overtalkative one, the silent
Jesus before Pilate; to one especially haunted by intellectual pride,
Jesus setting a little child before him. The suggestion is a useful one
at some stages of inner growth.

group, the silent presence of this member may exert more influence on the course of what is said than any of the speakers.

Have you ever tried to give a religious talk to a group of unemployed men? Peter Scott did this to a group of unemployed miners at Bryn Mawr in Wales—many of whom had been out of work for from seven to ten years. They said nothing back to him as he talked and talked. But their silence searched him, choked him, and at last reduced him to silence. He went away inwardly humiliated, but he returned soon to throw in his lot with theirs, to help them pool their capacity, to work and to rebuild their community on a basis of co-operative and self-help enterprises. Jane Addams knew what the presence of a silent one did to you. When she went out to talk about Hull House and its work to eager audiences, she often used to take with her some neighborhood woman who lived on Halsted Street and knew what Hull House was and was not doing. The woman only sat there silently through the speech, but she kept Jane Addams "close to the root."

In the silence of prayer such a silent one is present. He searches your many words and desires and opinions. There in the silence one comes under what Nicholas of Cusa in his important fifteenth-century devotional guide calls *The Gaze of God*. There we discover again that in a sunlit room every cobweb is visible and that under the searchlight of the operating room even the minutest canker is able to be seen. There we are stripped of all the pretensions of speech, there the perspective is restored. There we discover once more that we are what we are before God.

In the silence I may go on pressing my own justification. I may defend an act of dishonesty, or hatred, or cowardice, or compromise: after all, there are others far worse than I (oh blessed comparison); then, too, there were the circumstances which surely justified an exception being made (oh compassionate circumstance); at any rate it seemed so at the time even if it does not now; yes, it could be put right if I dared to admit what had been done; yes, it will be put right; give me the strength to carry this through; forgive, heal, unite us again; and then I, too, am silent in the company of the silent one.

Dostoevsky in the scene of the Great Inquisitor in the fifth book of *Brothers Karamazov* has given a great literary representation of this inner process. Jesus appears again on the pavement before the great cathedral in sixteenth century Seville. The very bricks in the plaza are still hot from the burning of a hundred heretics to the glory of God on the previous day. Once more Jesus begins to heal and to restore to life. He is instantly the center of a great rejoicing throng of the common people who recognize him. The cardinal inquisitor passes by, senses the situation, has Jesus arrested and put into a prison cell. That night the cardinal inquisitor visits the cell alone to face and accuse his prisoner: the silent Jesus. Why had he come now to hinder the work of the church? He had had his chance fifteen centuries before. He might have turned the very stones into bread and with bread to offer, all men would have followed him; he might have flung himself from the highest steeples and superstitious, mystery-hungry man would have delivered over his very soul to him; he might have assumed the power of authority and all men would have bowed to his might. Yet he had renounced all of these things: bread, dramatic mystery, outer authority—renounced them because he wanted only free men to be his companions, not slaves. Yet he has asked far too much of men. They did not want this freedom. They rejected it. And an historical institution, the church, sprang up that supplied miracle and mystery and authority, and men were satisfied.

Now why had he come again to hinder their work? Oh yes, as a young man, the cardinal went on to confess that he, too, had dreamed of the freedom to which men were called. But he saw that this was a mistake, an illusion. Now he *knew* men. Perhaps in some world, but here never! On and on, round and round, the cardinal talks and Jesus only listens in silence. Finally the cardinal can stand it no longer. He cannot bear the silent searching of those mild eyes. Anger he could deal with, but not such love. "Go and come no more! Come not at all, never, never, never!"

In Dostoevsky's scene the silent Jesus crosses and presses a loving kiss on the bloodless lips of the old Cardinal and leaves, to be seen no more. In prayer, he remains. If anyone leaves, it is yourself, because you are not yet ready to yield and to begin actively to respond. But the door of the cell is open. You may return at any hour of the day or night and he will be there.

Here is the silent confessional. Here is the center where the negative field is dispersed and where we discover the center of validity again. Here is where contrition is felt, restitution is seen, where future action is faced. This silent one, this indwelling Christ is what Isaac Penington meant when he wrote: "There is a pure seed of life which God hath sown in thee; oh that it might come through, and come over all that is above it, and contrary to it! And for that end wait daily to feel it, and to feel thy mind subdued by it, and joined to it. Take heed of looking out, in the reasonings of thy mind, but dwell in the feeling sense of life; and then that will arise in thee more and more, which maketh truly wise, and gives power, and brings into holy authority and dominion of life."

A friend who is one of the most effective clergymen in the middle-west has told me that, without entering into this silence each day of his life and opening up every pore of his life before God, the praise and eulogy and adulation which he as a clergyman is subject to would make a play-actor of him within a month. There in the silence this cloud of disproportion disperses and in the quiet he sees the true lines again. When he is under attack and criticism and once more his estimation of his work is subject to outward distortion, this time of silent prayer is equally important in restoring the true lines. In surface life we tend to be exclusively subjects to ourselves, whereas others are objects to us. In the silence this process is reversed and under God's gaze we become objects for ourselves and others are seen as subjects; i. e., as they see themselves. Dwight Morrow put this in another way when he suggested one time that we tend to judge ourselves by our ideals and others by their actions. To come under the gaze of God reverses this process. Nowhere is there any therapy that can induce a comparable objectivity toward the self or a comparable imaginative understanding of others.

Nothing contributes more to this objectivity than the gathering, the unifying, and the *simplifying* of the self that takes place in silent prayer. I once saw a manuscript on which an author was working when he died. The materials were all there, far more material than he could possibly have used. There was a rough preliminary outline and here and there a suggestive paragraph. But the mind that was to have brooded over this mass, this heap—the mind that would at some moment have seen a simple line dart through all of these materials, make most of them superfluous, underline the few remaining, and produce out of it all a living unity—this mind was withdrawn by death. And the manuscript remained only a confused heap.

Silent prayer simplifies the confused, complex, conflicting heap of life's experiences. It makes us one again. It restores us to the creative matrix. Augustine described its action with unerring directness when he wrote in his *Confessions,* "I collected myself from the dispersion in which I turned from Thee, the One, and was vainly divided." It is not so different from a man who has wandered into the woods and lost his way. After beating all night in the heavy under-brush, he sinks down toward morning; and there from the ground he sees ahead of him an open clearing and he slowly recognizes it to be one he knows well enough; and at last he knows where he is and what he has done and what he must do next. Before he saw this opening, all had been hope-lessly confused. Now it is simple and clear.

In silent prayer the many seems to give way to the one. Complexity seems to yield to simplicity. "He to whom the Eternal Word speaketh is delivered from many opinions." But it is no empty oneness that is accomplished there. There is a selection at work in silent prayer. Roiled water when allowed to settle becomes clear at the top. As a boy I used to watch my grandmother pour out the milk into broad flat pans and set these away on the shelf of the darkened milk room. For cream rises to the top when the milk is not disturbed. Robert Barclay, a seventeenth century Quaker, sensed this as he described the power of a group assembled in silent prayer: "As I gave way unto it, I found the evil weakening in me and the good raised up."

PRAYER OF PETITION

As we bear in mind the intense spiritual action upon us of this Divine *field of force* when we open ourselves to it, we may expect to approach the matter of asking for specific things in prayer—of petitional prayer with a better hope of understanding it.

There are those who look upon any specific request in prayer as a sign that the one who makes it is still at an in-

fantile level in prayer—that he still looks upon God as a
kind of a glorified Santa Claus to whom he sends up his
Christmas lists. To these persons, petition has no place in
mature prayer. "When I pray for aught, my prayer goes
for naught, when I pray for naught, I pray as I ought."
They would commend to us Thomas Aquinas' single petition when visited in prayer, and asked what he desired as
reward for his matchless writings in defense of God's cause:
"Naught but Thyself!" Often they remind us that God
knows our need before we utter it, and hence our petition
is superfluous.

It is impossible for me to face these difficulties without a
sense that they are not so real as they sound. Remembering
always the wise New Testament condition to insure participation and distinguish prayer from magic—"If ye abide in
me and my words abide in you, ye shall ask what ye will. . . ."
—remembering Jesus' inclusion of the element of petition
in the simple "Our Father" which he gave to the people,
and remembering his own free use of petition in his prayers
—our minds may be set somewhat at ease about being child-
like enough to use it freely. It is not a question of adding
to God's knowledge of our needs, nor is it a question of
"changing God's mind" by our request. To bring a specific
request into the silence and lay it before God is to enter
more deeply into the "Spiritual Combat." What I request
is a desire, or a longing or an aspiration that is a part of
me—whether it be good or evil. If I did not raise it in
prayer it would remain a part of me. If it was something
below my best it might go on increasing until it gained
control. If it was in keeping with my best and yet was never
brought into prayer, it might lack that confirmation that
would be the factor in its accomplishment.

If my life is to be lived as a friend of God, to be lived in
response to the discerning love of God, how can I do other

than to lay my desires and longing before Him for review and plead the case for them if I feel strongly about them? If I believe I love a girl, or if I am considering some undertaking whose success seems of great moment to me, where better could I take these matters than to prayer, where I may ask God to further them? That He will do so is another matter. I may beg with all my might for some outcome, and I may, after an hour, arise convinced that it is not to be, or that it must be in another form, or that I must wait, or that I must take this costly step in order for it to come about. It does not matter where or with what petitions we begin in prayer. *What is really important is where we end, where we are brought to in prayer.* The real question to ask of ourselves after prayer is: "Were you faithful? Did you yield?"

But what about prayers for rain? Those who ask this question usually set up a deep ditch between the *psychological* and the *physical* and insist that whereas prayer may affect the psychological, it may never cross the ditch to influence the physical. George Meredith insisted that we ought not to expect God to step in between us and the operation of His laws. In the healing of the sick, the boundaries of this ditch have changed somewhat since Meredith's time. Some physicians have begun to admit that what the patient believes profoundly affects his chances for physical recovery. This has not meant an abandonment of medical science. It has only been a recognition that body and mind are not enemies, but function as a whole, and that the structure of the "laws" that the human being responds to is broader than he, as a doctor, had formerly suspected. In fact the very status of physical laws is at no point so absolute or inexorable as Meredith and his generation believed it. Some of the ablest of scientists are willing to admit that science deals with reality in only one of several possible ways, each of which leave out something which could be known only by the adoption of a different approach.

We do not know that prayers for rain affect a power that supplies a factor left out by meteorological predictions. Neither do we know that this is not the case. In either event, it implies no abandonment of our active co-operation with our creative stem: the earth and the air—the conservation of moisture by the planting of forests, the plowing under of humus matter, the continuing to experiment with mechanical means of influencing the precipitation of moisture-laden clouds, the improvement of our techniques of irrigation. Prayer is only another form of this same intimate co-operation between us and the stem. If a group of people are suffering from a drought that threatens them with extinction and if they are people who hold up their every need in prayer, they can and should make no exception of this need. The boundaries of this ditch are yet to be established, and is there not the promise that if you abide in the life, "ye shall ask what ye will . . . "? There is, then, no absolute limit that can be placed upon petition. The only limit is man's need. But the prior condition must never be forgotten—the condition is to abide in Him and that His words shall abide in you. The condition is that you shall yield, that you shall respond, that you shall be faithful. Faith in God is set prior to faith in prayer, yet given this, you may begin at any point. And those old friends of prayer take their every need into prayer with great ease and confidence.

PRAYER OF INTERCESSION

Prayer for others is a form of petitional prayer that makes deep demands on the faith of an individualistic generation that has so largely lost its sense of inner community. Yet at no point do we touch the inner springs of prayer more

vitally than here.   For when we hold up the life of another
before God, when we expose it to God's love, when we pray
for its release from drowsiness, for the quickening of its
inner health, for the power to throw off a destructive habit,
for the restoration of its free and vital relationship with its
fellows, for its strength to resist a temptation, for its courage
to continue against sharp opposition—only then do we sense
what it means to share in God's work, in His concern;
only then do the walls that separate us from others go down
and we sense that we are at bottom all knit together in a
great and intimate family.   There is no greater intimacy
with another than that which is built up through holding
him up in prayer.   The firm bond that existed between
John Fredric Oberlin and his parish was laid each morning
in the hour that he devoted to prayer for his individual
parishioners.   We are told that as they went past his house
at this hour in the morning, they did so in quiet, for they
knew what was happening there.   Forbes Robinson's
Letters to His Friends reveal his constant use of this form
of prayer for his Cambridge associates.   He remarks in one
letter that if he would really reach some need in his friend's
life, he would always prefer a half-hour's silent petition for
him to an hour's conversation with him.

An unbeliever once mockingly begged Catherine of
Sienna that she pray for his soul.   She prayed by day and
by night, and the power of renovation disarmed and brought
him to his knees.   I know of a Japanese girl whose father
had found a whole chain of reverses too much for him to
meet normally and who had taken the alcoholic short-cut.
She prayed for him hour after hour until the time came
when he yielded, gave up drink, committed his life to the
center of Divine love he had experienced, and with the help
and love of his devoted family he has continued in a new
way of life.

It is not a question of changing God's mind or of exercising some magical influence or spell over the life of another. Before we begin to pray, we may know that the love of One who is actively concerned in awaking each life to its true center is already lapping at the shores of that life. We do not do it all. Such prayer is only co-operation with God's active love in besieging the life or new areas of the life of another, or of a situation. If you pray for something other than what is in keeping with that co-operation, you go against the grain, and if you remain in prayer and are sensitive, you will realize this and be drawn to revise it. As in all petitional prayer, he who really prays must be ready himself to yield.

You may pray for the release of some area of life in a friend and find that you are called upon to set right something in your own life that has acted as a stumbling block to him. You may pray that your friend be given courage to endure certain hardships and find that you are drawn to pack your bag and go and join him or that you are to give up your pocket money for the next month or even perhaps to give a fortnight or a month's salary to help along his cause. In intercessory prayer one seldom ends where he began.

During these active forms of work in the silence: in contrition, in purification, in simplification and refreshment, in petition, and in intercession, frequently if we are sensitive and listening, there come clear insights of things to be done. Often they come in that receptive silent waiting after we have opened our needs and where we do nothing but wait for direction. Again they may come during the day and push their way in between events that seem to bear no connection with them. These insights are precious and are to be heeded if we are to live in response to that which we feel in prayer. When they involve some real readjustments that may be costly to effect, the Quakers have called these *concerns*. They want a word for the tiny promptings, the gentle whispers that are equally as important and that may represent concerns in the forming.

"Prayer is incipient action," and these clues are the lines along which the molten freedom of the man in prayer are to be cast. *"Mind the light"* reads an inscription on a sundial. Come under holy obedience. Here is the unformed side of life's relationships—the letters to be written, the friends to be visited, the journey to be undertaken, the suffering to be met by food, or nursing care, or fellowship. Here is the social wrong to be resisted, the piece of interpretative work to be undertaken, the command to "rebuild my churches," the article to be written, the wrong to be forgiven, the grudge to be dropped, the relationship to be set right, the willingness to serve God in the interior court by clear honest thinking and the refusal to turn out shoddy work. Yet we need more than the intimations. We need spiritual staying power to carry them out. "Profession of truth, without the life and power, is but a slippery place, which men may easily slide from," wrote Isaac Penington. He commends his own practice of praying to be established in the power that will enable him to carry out these leadings. "I wait on Him for the strength to fulfill it." Here in the silence, as that power gathers, it is well to face the difficulty one will meet in carrying out this concern. Here in the silence it is well to see the only semi-inflammable character of the bridge you mean to burn; to face the inertia, the resistances, the amused smiles of friends; the coldness and want of understanding on the part of many who resent having their attention called to social injustice in which they are involved—the strangling doubts of your own later hours—doubts that led Theresa of Avila to say: "I see few

people who have not too much sense for everything they
have to do." These need to be met and overcome in the
silence.

If we ignore these leadings, they poison future prayer.
Katherine Mansfield wrote, "I went upstairs and tried to
pray, but I could not, for I had done no work." And if
they are ignored, they break the precious chain of influence
that this act may have set going. You become a link in this
chain when you begin to pray. If you fail, it must wait
for another. "Were you faithful? Did you yield?"

There is nothing greater than this constant fidelity. "The
world goes forward," wrote Harold Gray, who served a term
in Leavenworth during the war for his conscientious ob-
jection, "because in the beginning one man or a few were
true to the light they saw and by living by it enabled others
to see." Holy obedience to the insights, the concerns that
come, that persist, and that are in accord with co-operation
with God's way of love is not only the active side of prayer,
but is the only adequate preparation for future prayer.

There can be no complete prayer life that does not return
to the point from which we began—the prayer that is a response to the outpouring love and concern with which God
lays siege to every soul. When that reply to God is most
direct of all, it is called *adoration*. Adoration is "loving
back." For in the prayer of *adoration* we love God for himself, for his very being, for his radiant joy.

"Religion is adoration," was a favorite remark of that
veteran of prayer, Friedrich von Hügel. "The most funda-
mental need, duty, honour, and happiness of men is not
petition or even contrition, nor again, even thanksgiving . . .
these three kinds of prayer which indeed must never dis-
appear out of our spiritual lives, but *adoration*." Adoration
is not alone a special stage in prayer, although it may be
that, too. All the truest prayer is shot through with it and

its mood is the background to all real contrition, petition, and intercession.

In adoration we enjoy God. We ask nothing except to be near Him. We want nothing except that we would like to give Him all. Out of this kind of prayer comes the cry "Holy! Holy! Holy!" In the school of adoration the soul learns why the approach to every other goal had left it restless.

CHAPTER IV

THE PRACTICE OF CORPORATE WORSHIP

"At home, in my own house, there is no warmth or vigor in me, but in the church when the multitude is gathered together, a fire is kindled in my heart and it breaks its way through."—Martin Luther

THE NEED FOR CORPORATE WORSHIP

Remedy it as you will, it is a great misfortune to be brought up as an only child. The family constellation is too close, too concentrated, for either parent or child to receive a full appreciation of the other, or for the child to discover what it means to be at home, literally at home, with his fellows. At best, an only child has to learn outside the family, and outside its close circle of affection and common life, what it means to be one among others and to be a beloved one among others who are no less beloved, to learn how a mother's or a father's love is not divided when it is shared. And an only child seldom comes to know the parent's love as a child does who has seen it shared with his brothers and sisters and knows how dear each is to them. There are times in a large family of children when a child can and should be alone with the parent. But even these times are enhanced by the occasions when the child is with the parents in the midst of the family and as a member of the family.

Nowhere is this psychological truth better revealed than in the relation between private and corporate worship. For central as is the relationship between the separate individual and God, each man needs an experience of life in the great family of God if he is to grow to understand the real nature of that love and the real character of his response to that love, to say nothing of growing to understand and to live creatively with his fellows.

For the past fifteen years I have lived among students and intellectual people both in this country and abroad. And I have seen the pain and the blocking of inner growth that has come to people who have known the religious life, for the want of fellowship and of active participation in the corporate worship and family life of some religious group. The "only child" often turns into a kind of migratory religious tramp who floats from one church to another and only rarely stays long enough to become established in its form of corporate worship. It is not unusual for him to become disgusted with all forms of corporate worship and to take refuge in Professor Whitehead's well-known remark that religion is what a man does with his solitariness. Even this surface contempt, however, does not always conceal the lingering wistfulness in such a person for a religious fellowship.

Critical as this generation is, and may be justified in being, of the existing forms of religious fellowship, it can no longer be content with the emphasis of men such as William James, who interpreted religion as an individual affair that had little to do with its group expressions, or even with Henri Bergson, for whom the corporate side of religion can never be other than a static element. This Olympian aloofness of "sitting like God, holding no form of creed but contemplating all" and feeling above active participation in corporate worship has flatly failed to help its defenders to grow in the religious life. And no matter what form these religious associations may be destined to take in the future, they cannot be abolished entirely if religion is to live.

I know of a dozen young religious leaders in the East

between the ages of twenty-five and forty who constantly express to one another that they run down in the vital personal religion which they have at times discovered. With their connection with corporate worship for the most part very loose, and a certain sense of spiritual poverty about some of these institutional contacts, they are finding it ever so hard to get beyond that stage where they commenced their growth. As for the contagious communication of this spiritual life to others, it has changed from being central to being incidental with them. I think of a South American friend who has been alienated from his native church by a long-standing enmity and has been kept out of Protestantism by what he regards as its sectarian divisiveness and social apostasy. I think of a Danish friend who has given up the Danish Lutheran Church but can find fellowship in no other corporate worship. They are seeking to live the religious life alone. I see here the agony, the tragic loneliness, the cramping sense of martyred superiority, the hardening process of doubt about the validity of the whole spiritual life, and the temptation to be content with rational presentations of it which they would be the first to admit. In all of this I seem to see the sterilizing effect of religious individualism, of being God's "only child."

Lawrence Hyde, a young English critic of culture, has equally sensed this in his generation in England. "I suggest that the modern cultivated person is *over-estimating* his power of maintaining contact with the realm of the spiritual in his present condition. . . . He imagines in his self-sufficiency that he can get along satisfactorily without rites and ceremonies, without private disciplines, without associating himself on a religious basis with a group of his fellowmen. But the plain fact is that he cannot—unless he is a very exceptional person indeed. The great mass of more highly educated men and women today—those anyway of a more spiritual type—are psychologically unstable, restless, unfulfilled, and morbidly self-conscious."[1]

RELIGIOUS BEHAVIORISM

There is, in many, an aversion to entering into corporate worship because they do not feel worthy of all that it stands for or because they do not yet feel sure of their beliefs. I know how many go through struggles about partaking of communion because of their sense of unworthiness and want of complete conviction. They seem often enough to have forgotten Jesus' words, "They that are whole need not a physician, but they that are sick." A friend of mine went to a teacher in a religious seminary and told him that he had considered entering the seminary and training to be a minister but that he felt that he was unworthy to become a representative of Jesus Christ. He rather expected to be rallied. But to his secret dismay, the teacher agreed with him about his unworthiness and quietly suggested that if he ever felt otherwise, then he might seriously doubt his place in the church either as minister or parishioner.

Vida Scudder, the life-long champion of so many radical social causes, tells in her recent autobiography, *On Journey*, of her entrance into a lay Episcopal society: "The act did not mean that my religious vision had cleared; my faith was still provisional. But I was increasingly aware that, for me, rejection of what the Church offered would involve more falsity than acceptance. . . . Many thinking moderns who would like to be Christians spend their lives in a state of religious incertitude; we fall into two groups. Some, remaining poised in hesitation, including well-known minds I will not name, pause with imaginative and perhaps intellectual sympathy toward Christianity; others, passing be-

[1] *Prospects of Humanism*, p. 167 (Scribner).

yond theory, made the definite venture of faith, and seek less to know the doctrine than to live the life. Through the years of which I am now writing, I came, deliberately and with finality, to range myself on their side of the barrier."

The rôle that actual participation in corporate religious worship plays in nurturing the life of us halting ones has too long been obscured. Augustine's regular attendance on the church celebrations and the sermons of Bishop Ambrose in Milan played no small part in preparing him for that scene in the garden where he consciously yielded to the Christian way. Only in vital action, whether it be symbolic or direct, does thought ripen into truth, and the modern mind would do well not to confuse religion with a state of consciousness. "Thou art man," *The Imitation of Christ* gently reminds us, "and not God; Thou art flesh and no angel." And Pascal saw that this flesh must be disciplined not alone by thoughts but by acts of love and by corporate acts of worship. "For we must not misunderstand ourselves; we are as much automatic as intellectual; and hence it comes that the instrument by which conviction is attained is not (rationally) demonstrated alone." We become what we do. A great religious interpreter of our times once said that he kissed his child because he loved her and that he kissed his child in order to love her more. Regular participation in corporate worship is a school and a workshop in which those who would grow in the religious life, no matter how tenuous may be their present connections, should be in attendance.

CREATURELINESS AND SOCIAL RESPONSIBILITY

It is almost impossible to avoid a self-centered religion when one has no active regular share in the corporate worship of a larger religious fellowship. This is particularly true of those who are not engaged in manual work. There is the subtle temptation to become one of those who mistake being "agin" the group, being otherwise-minded, for following the dictates of conscience. Eccentricity, the sense of martyrdom, and an almost total absence of that precious element of "creatureliness," of humility in one's religious life as one of the great family of fellow creatures offering up their lives before the great Father—these frequently accompany this reluctance to share in corporate worship. Friedrich von Hügel used to tell of the sense of common need and of common love that came to him as he prayed through his rosary or listened to the mass while kneeling next to some Irish washerwoman. For this woman and millions of others, whatever their place in man's petty order of rank, would that very day perform the same act of love and devotion before a Father in whose loving regard each was of equal worth.

It is this vivid sense of creatureliness and the felt attitude of the creature towards the creator that many have declared to be the central experience of worship or devotion and the very secret source of the religious refreshment at the base of their lives. For in this sense of creatureliness, the springs of the only enduring center of equality between men are forever being renewed. Here is the heart of a social gospel that is eternal. Here each is visited with a sense that he, in his need, is one and only one among other needy ones; that he is one among the many who have come to offer up their adoration and aspiration; that he is responsible for all and can never wrench loose from that responsibility. Howard Brinton has expressed the effect of this approach to the center in the fellowship of worship by the figure of the spokes of a wheel. The nearer the spokes of the wheel are to the center, the nearer they are to each other. If the worship is real this new sense of nearness to others will invade the rest of life and be brought to work on the barriers which retard it there. Dean Sperry, in his *Reality in Worship,* has suggested that, if men were to cease to worship God, the greatest single incentive to fraternal ways among men would be withdrawn. For in such offices of worship addressed to God "the imagination is kindled, the heart is made catholic in sympathy and the good-will is fortified. ... Sincere and true thoughts of God are the strongest known nexus between man and man."

Fellowship and Nurture

Corporate worship, however, does much more than to induce creatureliness and to strengthen the bonds of the divine family. The regular participation in corporate worship nurtures the tender insight of private prayer and helps to give it a stalk, a stem, a root, and soil in which to grow. Without its strengthening power of believing in your conviction, you may be overcome by the general attitude of the world in which you live or by the same attitude that is being pressed upon you from within by the vast residue of fear-carcasses that the mind and habits are still laden with and that have not yet been cleared away. How many such personal "openings" have become mere pressed flowers in your book of memories for the want of a sensitive fellowship in which you might have recast your life and seen the next steps that were to be taken. In this fellowship you might have found others more mature in this life, from whom you could get counsel, and you might have found an association in which you could quicken some by your own discoveries. Not only in the tender beginning, but at every point in the life, we need this fellowship of corporate worship. For again and again, dry times and doubt and conflict level the fragile house of our faith and compel us to rebuild it on deeper foundations. At times the fellowship seems the only cord that holds us.

It is well not to ignore the fact that we are creatures of short memories. Corporate worship, regularly practised, calls us back again and again to the divine background and to our life that springs from it. We need a supernatural witness, a great sheet anchor for our souls. We need corporate encouragement to recall and be re-dedicated to that deep citizenship to which our lives stand pledged. To scorn such reminders and to claim all days as sabbaths and all places as equally holy may mean that one has reached a high sense of spiritual freedom. But it may also mean that one is approaching indifference. This corporate ceremonial communion in any Christian group that is more than occasional in its character carries a sense of historical continuity with a great spiritual tradition. You do not begin this quest nor will it end with you. It has been lived in the world of space and time by others who have gone before. Their lives have irrefutably proved and tested it and lifted it above the realm of speculative ideals and theories. It is no mean asset to have and to be regularly reminded of what T. S. Eliot calls "the backing of the dead." In such corporate worship you become a working member of that great community and you enter the vast company of souls whose lives are opened Godward. Your life takes on a new perspective in this great communion of the church invisible. This is not confined to the members of the historic churches but to any group that draws its life from the Christian stream, that possesses the biblical record, and that is sensitive to the witness of the saints.

WORSHIP AND ADORATION

But the deepest need in man which corporate worship ministers to has yet to be mentioned. If man is ever to rise to his full humanity, he must praise and adore that which is the highest that he knows and freely offer up to it the best that he has. The impulse in man to sacrifice to deity is primary in his nature. Even the great baboon solemnly bows again and again to the rising moon. Primitive man tremblingly prostrates himself before the sacred grove. The shepherd brings the most perfect lamb of his flock to be sacrificed on a rude heap of stones. The farmer brings to the priest his best sheaf of grain or a cruse of the finest oil from his grove of olives. The widow brings her mite. The Massachusetts pilgrim family tramps through the forest to the rude log church to kneel and sing and pray. The Pennsylvania Quaker family gathers with others in the plain stone meeting-house to sit in silent prayer and fellowship. The Maryland Catholic family enter the little chapel to share in the celebration of the mass and to donate themselves, as there is dramatized before them the sacred pageant of a self-donating God. Here is the operativeness of the same magnetic field on all of these differently sensitized dials. Here is what Hans Denck and after him Pascal sought to make explicit by their "you would not have sought Him if you had not already found Him."

No one can deny that in primitive man (and in that considerable substratum of the primitive that dwells in all of us) this longing to offer up the best that he has, to the highest that he knows, is often overlaid with fear and with the desire to propitiate or gain favors from the power or powers beyond his control. Yet even this cannot blind us to this basic longing in men to praise and to adore and to pour out their best gifts. For this longing persists after these fears or cravings for favors have been almost wholly stripped away. It is this longing in man that makes him God-man. It is this restlessness with the most secure self-sufficiency he can devise; it is this urge within himself to put himself in second place, to prostrate himself before the holiest of all, that is the hope in him. Deny man the right to offer himself to this as the saints have done; destroy his monuments of devotion, his cathedrals, his paintings, his carvings, his organizations for good works; ridicule his aspiration as infantile; try, in short, to roof over his sundial; try to choke out this longing to yield to Deity or to divert it to exclusively social aims—and man ceases to be man and something of his essence goes dead in him. Man is a praising and adoring being. He longs to celebrate all of his common experiences and to lift them up to a higher love by dedicating them. God bless my tools. It is because he spoke authoritatively to this center in men that they recognized the authenticity of Jesus and his message. It was because Jesus, too, praised and adored and fell down before his Father that they knew him to be flesh of their flesh and bone of their bone.

From the beginning of recorded history, religious institutions and the priesthood in nurturing and ministering to this basic human need have all too frequently preyed upon, perverted, prostituted, and misled this impulse in man. It is not insignificant that, with all of their betrayals, this longing in man to praise and to adore has persisted. And again and again it has purified itself.

THE WORSHIPER'S SHARE

There is no denying the fact that if you are to become a responsible member of any one of the existing religious groups, it will have to be to this power of inner purification that you must look for your hope, rather than to any present perfection. For whatever "the Church" may be, certainly "the churches" are not the pure leaven. They are a part of the loaf in which the leaven is active. Yet in our day the inner needs of men are compelling each church to learn something from the others and the purification is going on. This is especially noticeable in the free Protestant churches, where the deepest concern is being expressed over the manner in which they have tended to focus all upon the prophetic sermon to the neglect of praise and adoration.

It is no architectural accident that in their churches the pulpit and its occupant is usually placed squarely in the center of the platform. When the Mansfield College Congregational Chapel at Oxford, England, was being built, the proposal to return to the pre-reformation custom of having the altar in the center and the pulpit at the side drew a storm of protest from the great preacher-theologian Dale. He saw it as an attempt to dishonor the function of preaching and he felt the building to be scarcely fit for its main purpose.

There have been several major effects of this centering upon the sermon. One has been to regard all that precedes and follows it as a kind of opening and closing exercise, even though it might not be good taste to use these words. Another has been that since preaching was the backbone of the service, and since its appeal was to the reason and to moral sensitivity, the attender has found it quite natural to take up the same critical attitude toward the service that would be assumed in the courtroom or the lecture hall. The mind that listens, therefore, has tended to be tuned to argue and dispute, and in response to an inquiry about the service, a critical analysis of the preacher's arguments or of the quality of his oratory is almost sure to be given. Closely linked with this is the passive attitude which the attender readily slips into where he says in essence, "Well, here I am, now what have you got to offer?"

Søren Kierkegaard in his penetrating devotional address, *Purity of Heart*, describes this attitude by suggesting that most Protestant church attenders act as if the church were a theater, where they are the critical audience and where the minister is the actor whose art they are expected to enjoy and to criticize. The situation in a church where the attenders have found their real relationship, Kierkegaard points out to be a very different one. The stage is there still, but now the attenders are upon it. They are the actors. The audience is there too—God is the audience. The preacher is there also, but he is inconspicuous in the scene. He is only the prompter. He is behind the wings whispering the text that they as the actors are speaking aloud before God. The responsibility has shifted here, and the relation between preacher and congregation has shifted too. They are collaborators now. He is their helper. He furnishes a text by which they may examine themselves before God. Here is a new attitude toward worship. It has become an occasion for coming more consciously into the presence of God and of reviewing our lives under His loving scrutiny.

Yet this does not exhaust the direction in which this purification of the free Protestant worshiper's attitude may with profit be revised. For worship in its essence is also a time of praise, of thanksgiving, of adoration. Who would not go far to express his gratitude to a friend and to have a time of intimate fellowship with him? Whether others went in great numbers would not affect our desire to go, if there were a close bond between us. In a Roman Catholic church, mass is celebrated and God worshiped whether a congregation appears or not. If a worshiper has felt this inward drawing, he will not talk seriously of substituting the hearing of a radio-sermon for the fellowship of praise and worship any more than a lover would choose a telephone call when he had an opportunity to see and be with his beloved. And once in the service, the whole attitude is another one if the worshiper comes there in company with his fellows to pray, to praise, to thank, to adore, to examine himself before God with the help of the sermon. Now he is there not to get but to give. Now he sings the hymns to God, he shares vicariously in the public prayer, and as the minister speaks he may pray that his words may keep close to the root. If the sermon does not speak to his condition, he simply goes on praying inwardly and is not disturbed, knowing that perhaps another may be helped by precisely these words. Even a few such worshipers change the whole tone of the service.

This difference in attitude on the part of the worshiper, however, can neither be cultivated nor sustained unless it is accompanied by more opportunity in the free Protestant service for inward prayer, more congregational participation, closer fellowship among the members, and the readiness on the part of the minister to recognize that he does not do it all, but that he, in his need, joins with his congregation in this corporate act of rededication and praise. This humbler conception of the function of the preacher as a fellow of his people is well put by E. Shillito and does not exclude the work of the prophetic teacher: "He does not preach himself, and he is not, therefore, at the mercy of his own moods, or even of his experience. He is not compelled to preach only what he has made his own perfectly; he can turn the eyes of his people to Christ, whose riches are unsearchable. He is releasing a power of which he knows something, of which neither he nor any man can know all."[2]

In the Roman Catholic church, this basic longing in men and women to praise and adore has always been nurtured by the mass, which symbolizes Christ's sacrifice. The priest faces the altar, which is erected in Christ's honor and bears on it the crucifix. Except for intervals when the priest turns to evoke the responses of the worshipers, the whole service is directed not man-wards, but God-wards. Yet, for

---

[2] *Christian Worship*, edited by N. Micklem, p. 222 (Oxford).

all of the beauty and power of the service, there is in all liturgical forms of this character a tendency not only for a gulf to exist between the priest and the congregation, but for the worshipers to let the priest do the celebrating while they remain passively in attendance. Also, the social implications of this act of worship have too often been neglected. Under the pressure of the present circumstances in Germany, the church as a Christian family is appearing again, and the worshiper is being drawn more actively into praise. The priest often comes down to an altar in the nave among the worshipers to celebrate the mass; old liturgies are being revived in which the congregational responses play a large rôle in the service; and, in their need, they are reviving an early Christian practice of bringing bread and vegetables and grain and laying them on the altar rail as their gift to Christ when communion is taken. These gifts are later distributed among those in the greatest need. A whole school of Catholic thinkers have been concerned to show the deeper social implications of liturgy and to link, as Jesus did, the adoration of God with the love and corporate responsibility for my neighbor.

At the very time that the free Protestant denominations are concerned to restore to its true function the place of praise and adoration, and the Roman Catholic church shows signs at least of becoming more congregational and awakening to its prophetic function, it is interesting to look at the Quakers, whose silent meeting furnishes a third distinctive type of corporate service of worship. Here the Friends gather and sit in silent prayer. There are no ministers or priests. The worshiper is entirely free to enter into the seeking after "a holy dependence of the mind on God" or to sit apathetically by. The entire responsibility rests upon him. Now and then some member feels drawn to break the silence and share some message. For those who actively participate in this form of corporate inward prayer, there is often a melting down, a tendering, in which each feels very closely knit to the common Father and to his fellows. I have seen this silent worship level a group in which there was an ugly barrier separating two of its members, and I have seen it bring them to ask forgiveness. I have seen it prepare members in a group to enter into holy obedience against their surface wills on matters in which the whole future course of their lives were at stake. I have seen it as the occasion when in truth the group enjoyed God and could scarcely contain itself for thanksgiving. Yet today the Quakers are continually concerned for the prophetic teaching ministry of the word that the free Protestants would supplement, and as they look at the Catholic church they become acutely conscious of how little they are a communion of "all the people," of how few of the poor, the unwashed, the dispossessed they include in their membership.

Each of these characteristic types of corporate worship is being influenced by the genius of the other. Yet all who are conscious of their task as a Christian fellowship in the increasingly urbanized Western World recognize one common need that they must meet. Outside of the single hour of worship on Sunday, there is too little realization of vital interdependence among members of the religious communions to make the worship engage them sufficiently. They rarely share one another's hospitality any longer. They seldom take a hand at building a place of worship together where the personal labor of each is gayly given.

When the monks of Maria Laach, a German Benedictine abbey, worship together, and when they give one another the kiss of Christian peace, it means something. For at each point in their day—whether they are among those who work in the fields, or on stone or wood or canvas in the atelier, or in the research library of liturgical studies, or in conducting a retreat, or in the school, or in the kitchen—they are actively conscious of working for God and one another, and of participating in a state of mutual interdependence as members of a Christian family. A similar experience is had by members of some of the volunteer summer work-camps when they gather early in the morning for twenty minutes of silence before going off to a full day of hard physical labor on a common project that they are doing for the community. They are knit together and to the community and to the wider community of men because they have experienced this sense of vital interdependence in their local life outside of the specific acts of worship. The presence of small active Christian fellowships within the religious organizations themselves in which common work can be undertaken is an immediately valuable step. The indictment that the intensity of this very need throws upon the character of our urban life points to the need for far more profound alterations ahead.

Man's inner need for corporate religious fellowship, however, remains constant through all these transformations. And one who would grow in the religious life will do well to find which of the imperfect religious associations best meets this need for him and to become a living cell within it.

CHAPTER V

DEVOTIONAL READING

"To read not to contradict and confute."—Francis Bacon

There is a sense in which offering a chapter on the subject of devotional literature seems both superfluous and futile. Superfluous, for when you are really brought low, you will be compelled to seek out devotional literature for yourself and will have no need for the stimulus that such a chapter might yield. And futile, because until that time, the mere reading of such a chapter is not likely to make you a consistent reader of devotional literature. It can justify its inclusion only in the belief that this is addressed to those who are already "on journey," and that it may confirm some of their experiences and, like the asterisks in a Baedeker, perhaps suggest some treasure that in their own travels they had never thought of looking out.

There is a line in *The Imitation of Christ* that has consoled more than one hard-pressed student as he faced his examinations: "Truly in the day of judgment, we shall not be examined as to what we have *read* but as to what we have *done*. . . ." Yet if we look into the daily regimen of the men and women who seem to us to be growing in the religious life, we shall seldom find them neglecting to read nor failing to acknowledge that what they have read has profoundly influenced what they have done. Baron Friedrich von Hügel, the spiritual master of so many in this generation, wrote to a friend, "I have been so hard-worked that, for this kind of reading, I can only find my usual quarter of an hour, which has to go to those few books [Bible, and *The Imitation* (of Christ) and *Confessions* (of Augustine)] which have been my staple spiritual food hitherto." Henry T.

Hodgkin, the first director of Pendle Hill and another of the spiritual guides of our times, always "had some spiritual reading going," as he put it, and gave himself to it before the day's round began.

Not all lawyers emulate Sir Thomas More. Yet I happen to know two of the ablest legal minds in Philadelphia who are the most eager readers of devotional works and who find this nurture an imperative in keeping inwardly fresh and sensitive. These men are hungry. They are conscious of need and they are not too proud to ask for help. Close friends of mine ask one another, "What do you feed on?" "Where are you finding light?" "Who has pointed you most directly to what is real?" They want bread, not a diet of hors d'oeuvres. They want to be directed, not diverted. They are becoming less interested in reading about religion and religious controversy than in reading works that have sprung out of the religious response to life and hence that minister to it in themselves. In short, they are in search of books that will strengthen, increase, and intensify devotion. And devotion, we recall, means the "promptitude, fervor, affection, and agility" in our response to the burning ray of love that attends us. Here there is a longing for voices that speak of discovery, of its way, and of its object.

"We want someone," writes Lawrence Hyde, "who by the very nature of his being can confirm us in our more lofty and transient realizations, reinforce our weak and uncertain aspirations, recall to us the peace that passeth all understanding. . . . People do not read this *sacred* literature today: they are too 'emancipated'. . . . They will read Dostoevsky with avidity—chiefly because he lived a large part of his time in Hell, with the topography of which they are themselves perfectly familiar. But they forget that Dostoevsky himself was a passionate student of the New Testament. They are sensationalists; they want strong, rich meat, and find the dry bread of true spiritual teaching unassimilable. Yet I am bold to suggest that they will discover in the end that they cannot afford to dispense with it. . . . It is not going too far to suggest that every individual who pursues his search for spiritual illumination with sufficient persistence finally finds himself obliged to leave secular literature behind him. He must sit at the feet of those who, even if they are less sympathetic figures, owe their authority to the fact that they are standing, on more elevated ground. He must study scripture."[1]

How many times one has laid the *Bible* aside in favor of what seemed more real and compelling or more attractive and readable witnesses to the religious life, only to be driven back to it again by the great hunger. When one comes back under this need he does not set himself a rule to read religiously ten verses or two chapters a day. He does not use the *Bible* as a quotation dictionary in which a pithy text may be sought out that will gather up and fittingly decorate a sermon that he has already written. He is not content merely to search out favorite passages in order to let the measured dignity and beauty of their language stir in him an emotion like that which comes in listening to classical music or in seeing a finely proportioned building. Nor does he come to one of the gospels with the intent of ferreting out the delicate masonry with which the author has built on the early source manuscript "Q." He is ready "to read not to contradict and confute." He comes *open.* He comes to find something that will speak to his condition. He is searching for something that will interpret for him the meaning of the experience he has just had or the choice that lies immediately before him.

He reads, perhaps in one of the four gospels or in the

---

[1] *Prospects of Humanism,* pp. 161-163 (Scribner).

Psalms or in Isaiah, but now with eyes that see and that often leave him and his problem behind, seemingly swallowed up in oblivion and forgotten, for he has become absorbed in the majesty of another's life and teaching. He may lay the book aside and go on about his work or quite naturally move from it into prayer. It has quieted him, cleansed him, refocused his perspective, nourished him, and left him steady.

Another time as he reads he comes to a line or a word that seems written for no one in the world so specifically as for him. The word is tipped with an acid that eats through the toughest armor plate of defense and burns through the flesh to the vital part in him. When Augustine *took* and *read* in that Milan garden, his eye came upon words that revealed him to himself and left him God's captive—"defenseless utterly." When Francis of Assisi sat in the little Portiuncula chapel and heard those words read from the evangelist side of the altar, "Take nothing for the journey, neither stick nor wallet, nor bread, nor silver and do not carry two shirts," he knew that he had found his rule. The words for him bore the divine accent. He saw that they were intended for him.

This experience is not uncommon among those who read the Bible today. As they read, again and again a word is spoken in them and to them that reveals them to themselves. This honest generation is often reticent to give any verdict upon what is meant by revealed scriptures. But some of its members are not unfamiliar with what is meant by the Bible as a *revealing* scripture. And they know, too, that it is not alone the literal meaning of the words written there. For they may have read the identical passage a hundred times before and it had no more than a general meaning for them. "For many years I read much and understood nothing," wrote Theresa of Avila. But there came a day, and that when she was already thirty-nine years of age, when she began to understand more and more, and when she was fed, confirmed, strengthened, and led on by what she read.

Why did this revealing word not come before? Thomas Fuller, a seventeenth century divine, wrestled with this question: "Lord, this morning, I read a chapter in the Bible, and therein observed a memorable passage whereof I never took notice before. Why now, and no sooner did I see it? Formerly my eyes were as open, and the letters were as legible. Is there not a thin veil laid over Thy Word, which is more rarefied by reading and at last wholly worn away? I see the oil of Thy Word will never leave increasing whilst any bring an empty barrel."

Here is a straw of hope for the patient persevering reader! But had Thomas Fuller turned his attention to the none-too-thin veil of timidity, lethargy, and preoccupation that is laid over the will of the reader, he might have come even nearer to that veil that must be rarefied and worn away before the eyes may be truly open. It must be worn away not only by continued reading but by the coincident work of the invisible companion who acts upon us at each instant of our lives. Upon the occasion of our life experiences of joy, of suffering, of creating, of failure, of trust kept, of betrayal, steadily and without a shadow of turning, this presence haunts us, pulverizes our pretenses, heals our bruises, draws on our partial responses, and waits for us to awaken and respond to the *Everlasting Mercy* and pray:

> "O patient eyes that watch the goal
> O ploughman of the sinner's soul
> O Jesus, drive thy coulter deep
> To plough my living man from sleep."

Here is the preparation that, when we willingly yield to it, can wear away the veil and open the eyes of the soul to understand the next step as we marry our minds to revealing scripture. But reading the Bible without yielding to this preparation and without following out the light that comes is not likely to mean much. For revealing writing shares its treasures progressively and only at a price. Things have to be done. This revelation imposes upon the reader the condition that he open his life to it. It exacts a willingness on his part to let go his tense, tightly-clenched efforts at inner security, and a willingness to let the angel freely trouble the waters of his life to his healing. "In our earthly category of existence, there can be no disinterested knowledge of the content of revelation," wrote Karl Heim, "hence no close fellowship with Christ short of following after him. . . . Christ wants not admirers but disciples." But for one who is in growth, and is seeking to yield, the Bible becomes an indispensable companion because it does reveal the way and because it seems to point beyond to infinitely more of the same source of light which he has already experienced.

The cloud of witnesses and teachers, however, did not end at the close of the first century. And those who seek for nurture in the religious life are acutely conscious of the fact that revelation is continuous. It has never stopped. A reading of the *Selected Letters of Friedrich von Hügel* or of Evelyn Underhill's *Concerning the Inner Life* or *The Golden Sequence,* to mention only two names of writers in the English language, will convince almost any seeker that new and authentic voices have appeared even in our own generation. And in the eighteen intervening centuries a whole row of rich classics have appeared. They will not all speak to the needs of each person who reads them. We often find real companions who are to be cultivated by long intimacy, only at the end of a considerable search, a search that we must make for ourselves.

Take the *Confessions of Augustine.* There are some who will never respond to the Augustinian type, but who seek a

gentler guide whose twice-born character is not so sharply
to the fore. There are others who have not enough historical imagination and patience to abide the somewhat
extended narrative of postponed obedience that Augustine
gives in the first nine books of his *Confessions*. If they
could have a *Reader's Digest* book-summary that might include a record of his sins, the garden scene, and perhaps the
matchless description of his experience of wordless communion with his Mother at Ostia, they would eagerly read
it. There are anthologies that provide this for them and
that are not to be despised. But the more patient reader,
who will read these nine books or chapters (remembering
always that devotional books can never be read by those
who are in a hurry), will not go unrewarded. For the joy
of coming upon a passage for yourself, of discovering it,
of being discovered to yourself by it, perhaps of setting it
down in a notebook of quotations that you would go back
to again and again, or at least of marking it in the margin,
of stopping and dwelling upon it—there is something here
that is its own reward.

If you have never read Augustine in this way you have
probably failed to discover how readily and how naturally
the writer of a devotional book can flow from precise description into the most passionate prayer and then on into
narrative again without any note of artificiality whatever.
And you might also have missed sensing for yourself the
fact that this is so because the greatest of these devotional
classics have come out of the lives of men for whom prayer
and work, especially the work of writing or speaking, were
as intimately connected as that. Aquinas's long vigils before his appearances in public disputation, Pascal's declara-
tion that much of his *Thoughts* were written "on his knees,"
Søren Kierkegaard's words of his vocation as a writer: "I
have literally lived with God as one lives with a Father,

Amen. . . . I rise up in the morning and give thanks to God. Then I begin to work. At a set time in the evening I break off and again give thanks to God. Then I sleep. Thus do I live." These only confirm what you sensed at first hand as you read the *Confessions* of Augustine.

Only the patient reader can follow the slow emancipation of this strong, proud, self-willed man from the slavery of an inner paralysis, induced by conflicting desires, to a freedom that he called the *libertas major:* where you love God with all your heart and soul and mind, and are free to *do* as you then please. Only such a reader will learn of the way in which one by one Augustine was stripped of the evasions by which he illustrates his theme of the fugitive from God; of the successive development of his thought life up to a spiritual philosophy that at least would not impede belief; of the way in which his conversion was influenced by the examples of others: of Monica, of the deceased friend of his youth, of Victorinus, of St. Anthony, of Ambrose, and at last by that of the two young courtiers. There are few readers for whom this specimen of the death struggle between the Christian "obsession" and the restless mind and spirit of decadent fourth-century Roman culture will not yield insights into the faithfulness of the divine companion, the responsibilities and privileges of parenthood and friendship, the influences of thought systems, and the blessedness of decision and commitment.

Bernard of Clairvaux's *On Consideration* is likely to become the friend of those who have, or expect to have, administrative posts where the heavy responsibilities of control over others and where the whirl of affairs threaten to disperse them. Bernard wrote it for Eugenius III, a member of his own Cistercian order, who in 1145 was elected pope. Bernard, the counselor of kings and popes, knew from his own life both the disasters and the opportunities connected with exalted position. Much has been written on how to bear suffering and adversity, but rarely has anyone been concerned to help us learn how to carry what the world calls prosperity, and to keep the soul fresh and free under it. It is not easy to wear the high mantle lightly and to the service of one's colleagues. This cloak often sticks to the back and makes the manner stiff. Bernard's pithy counsel and deep insight are applicable today.

The *Little Flowers* of Francis of Assisi are read and re-read by those who seek the companionship of one who in the judgment of many was the "thirteenth disciple." In Francis we have the confirmation of Lawrence Housman's remark that "a saint is one who makes goodness attractive." In this quaint collection of folk-tales about Francis, known as the *Little Flowers,* the miracle-seeking Italian peasant mind has responded to the impression that the saint made upon it. The result is this collection of tributes to one who loved all creatures and all nature in the Father and Creator. Thomas Traherne's *Centuries of Meditations,* which sprang out of seventeenth-century England, is marked by this same temper of creation-love.

In the Christian world the most widely used manual of devotion outside of the Bible itself is *The Imitation of Christ.* Thomas à Kempis assembled and issued *The Imitation* in 1427 and again in a final edition in 1441. The most recent Dutch scholarship is convinced that nearly all of its text was taken directly from *The Spiritual Diary* of Gerard Groote, the founder of the Brethren of the Common Life, and that it is poured directly out of the stages of his own experience. The book is tinged with an ascetic note of how the body and the senses may best be kept under. Yet it is so packed with tried quotation and with the sound experiential wisdom of this great fourteenth-century Dutch layman that for five centuries it has met the devotional needs of men and women in every Christian communion. It has helped men and women prepare for death as well as life, and in 1915 Nurse Edith Cavell's well-scored copy of *The Imitation* was found in her cell after she was shot as a spy in Belgium.

Pascal's *Thoughts,* along with the New Testament, was the book the French soldier most often chose to take with him to the front in the last war as he went up to face death. Had Pascal lived, this collection of brilliant epigrams, aphorisms, and fragments were to have been expanded into a great *Apology* for the Christian religion. Many have found in the *Thoughts* a hint of the way along which the riddle of life and of what to do with life was to be resolved.

The young Luther's favorite devotional book, apart from the Bible and Augustine, was the *Theologia Germanica.* It was written about 1350 by the "Warden of the House" of the Teutonic Order in Frankfurt, who, like so many of the devout fourteenth-century Friends of God, chose to keep his name unknown. Rufus M. Jones tells us that no less than ninety editions of it were issued in Germany up to 1929. It is the testament of one who is concerned to draw our attention to what God is doing in us and who writes of his aspiration: "I would fain be to the Eternal Goodness, what His own hand is to a man."

Of the many devotional books that sprang out of the sixteenth-century counter-reformation in Spain and France, four may be mentioned here: Ignatius Loyola's *Spiritual Exercises* have been the model for Jesuit retreats and training, and no one can read them without learning much that will assist him in his own spiritual training. They are the work of a converted soldier who would make obedient soldiers of Jesus. Their grasp of human psychology is profound. Our generation is waiting for someone who is less concerned with regimentation to match for us Ignatius

Loyola's contribution to the training and discipline of the Christian life.

Theresa of Avila's *Autobiography* sheds much wise counsel as it tells, in a human way, the story of her life experience. Scupoli's *Spiritual Combat* is a stinging challenge in the form of a manual that quickens our conscience and stirs us into life on many fronts.

My own judgment is that for the day-to-day use of one living in the present world, none of these three quite approaches Francis de Sales' *Introduction to the Devout Life.* "Those who have treated of devotion have almost all . . . taught a kind of a devotion which leads to complete withdrawal. My intention is to instruct those who live in towns, in households, at the court; who very often, under color of an alleged impossibility, are not willing even to think of undertaking to live the devout life because they are of the opinion that . . . no one ought to aspire to the palm of Christian piety, while living in the midst of the press of worldly occupations. I show them that . . . [the] constant soul can live in the world. It is true that this is not an easy task and for this reason I should like many to undertake it with more zeal than has been shown up to the present."

Francis de Sales is still the model of a great school of directors of souls in the Roman Catholic and the Anglican churches. In this gem of devotional literature he pours out his counsel. The little volume has come out of long experience in the confessional, which, together with his own experience, taught Francis de Sales how to deal with men and women on the level where they live. It is packed with anecdote and analogy and is remarkably fresh today. The nature of the life of devotion, instruction in prayer and meditation, a consideration of the obstacles to prayer, how to remedy anger, of gentleness toward ourselves, of true friendship, marriage, society and solitude, of detraction from the good names of others—these are glimpses of the range of this book which almost any practising Christian will be poorer for neglecting. Fénelon's well-known *Spiritual Letters to Men* and *Spiritual Letters to Women;* Père Grou's *Manual for Interior Souls* to which von Hügel acknowledged so great a debt; and in our own time, Paul Claudel's *Letters to a Doubter* all stand in this same tradition of the spiritual counselling of individual souls. Von Hügel's writings have already been mentioned. His *Letters to His Niece* and *The Life of Prayer* are admirable little volumes to begin on. Forbes Robinson's *Letters to His Friends* is perhaps the most convincing modern statement of the power of intercessory prayer.

In the same century that Francis de Sales published his *Introduction to the Devout Life,* George Fox took advantage of his extended periods of leisure in English jails to set down a record of his experiences in what we know as his *Journal.* George Fox tells of his struggle to find what was real; of the blind alleys he encountered in his search; and of his discovery that there was one who could speak to his condition and that that one dwelt within him—the inward Christ, the inward light. He tells of his scrupulous attempt to follow that light and to be "bottomed" in it; of how the inner logic of that light led him to recognize it in others and made it perfectly natural for him to renounce an offer of a captaincy in Cromwell's army because of living "in the virtue of that life and power that took away the occasion of all wars." Or he tells of how naturally he was led to petition the judges for fairer wages for the servant classes, to appeal to the government for a plan of public works to relieve unemployment, or to urge the gentle and brotherly treatment of the red Indian. Here the nurture of the personal religious life is not neglected. Yet out of that stillness and coolness of mind that he counseled came a radical ethic of love that was not wanting in power and that inspired the early Society of Friends that Fox called together.

A century later, John Woolman, a tailor who lived in Mt. Holly, New Jersey, set down in his *Journal* the record of another life that bears this same stamp of tenderness and concern for his fellow-creatures. After reading this *Journal*, few would hesitate to declare that they had discovered the American saint of the eighteenth century—few could shake off his influence upon them. In the *Journal* is found the intimate life of the man who as early as 1742 was enlarged by this growing tenderness and reverence for the light of God in others and was led to see the incongruity and inherently debasing influence on owner and slave alike of the whole slavery system. But it did not rest with seeing. Step by step, the *Journal* shows how this led first to that difficult *local* action that is necessary to test an insight, and then on to wider responsibilities. Married and with a wife and daughter to maintain, Woolman revealed how *concerns* can be carried out and responsibilities also met if one is ready to simplify demands and live "a life so plain that a little suffices."

The *Journal* tells of how he simplified and cut down his business until he could be spared from time to time to make the journeys he felt called to undertake. It tells of his work, which is known to have aroused the Society of Friends and led it to clear itself of slave owning by the close of the Revolutionary War. There is a record of the searchings of conscience about taxes that might be used in support of the military during the French and Indian War, and of how Woolman risked his life to go to Western Pennsylvania on a mission of love to a group of Indians at a time when the Indian population at large had been driven to violent retaliation by the ill treatment they had received from the whites. His account of the frequent renewings of inner refreshment that came to him as he kept "close to the root," his testimony for simplicity, his identification with those who suffer injustice, and his method of approach to those with whom he differed and hoped to win, make John Woolman's *Journal* a testament of insight for those who are seeking light on the rôle of the Christian layman in the social dilemmas of our day. Dawson's *Life of John Fredric Oberlin* gives an account of the discipline of life of a French Protestant contemporary of Woolman who in a spiritual, social, and economic sense literally made over a community in the Vosges mountains in Alsace by fifty years of continuous service there.

Here and there in devotional literature a piece of writing appears that so far as we may know was never meant to be seen by any other eyes than the writer's own. Lancelot Andrewes: scholar, courtier, privy-council member, preacher, controversialist, Bishop in Shakespeare's and Francis Bacon's England, set down in the solitude that he wrung from his heavy responsibilities a manual of prayers and forms of examining his own conscience. Since they were only for his own use, he wrote them down in Greek, in Latin, or in Hebrew, and he used them constantly in the hours he spent in prayer. On his death bed he gave a copy to his dear friend, Bishop William Laud, for his use. No publication of them was ever intended, nor did it follow officially until almost fifty years after Andrewes' death. A century and a half later John Henry Newman sought to recover the *Private Devotions of Lancelot Andrewes* for nineteenth-century England by translating the Greek portions into English. In these prayers the curtain of this saint's life is drawn aside. I know of no writing in which the prayers of confession, of intercession, and of thanksgiving have such a consistently true ring as there. To read

them aloud is to be pricked into confession, to learn how to
intercede, and to be inflamed into thanksgiving. It is also
to learn how precious an exercise it is to prepare for yourself a set of devotions that speak precisely to your own needs.
Frank Carleton Doan's *Eternal Spirit in the Daily Round*
and John Baillie's recent *Diary of Private Prayer* both bear
the marks of such a birth. They would have been more
than justified if thousands of others had never been given
the boon of being permitted to read them, but if they had
been searched out and set down solely out of the writer's
own needs and upsurgings of heart in order to help him
come nearer to God in his private worship.

"Sacred Literature," to use Lawrence Hyde's term, does
not, however, exhaust the materials that may be used in
devotional reading. Some find that great religious poetry
opens doors for them that no manual of devotion can un-
fasten. George Herbert, Robert Herrick, John Donne,
Thomas Traherne, Blake, Shelley, Wordsworth, Browning,
Tennyson, Coventry Patmore, Francis Thompson, Gerard
Manley Hopkins, and Robert Bridges are a few of the names
of those whose poems have quickened and fed the lives of
many. The *Oxford Book of Mystical Verse* has no serious
rival today as an anthology of the religious writings of most
of these men.

Well-chosen biography is another source of reading that
quickens devotion. This is especially true of that period
in life when a life-work is being chosen, although there are
few periods in later life when such a book may not deepen
the life vocation of one already established. Allen's
Phillips Brooks for the ministry; Cushing's *Life of William
Osler* (which one of my friends described as "the most religious book I have read in years") for medicine; Schweitzer's
Out of My Life and Thought for those who would see how
a vocation of musician, physician, and theologian need not

be mutually exclusive; George Herbert Palmer's *Life of Alice Freeman Palmer* for the work of education; Janet Whitney's *Elizabeth Fry* for the work of social reform; Rufus M. Jones's three little autobiographical volumes called *Finding the Trail of Life* or Bliss Perry's *And Gladly Teach* that tell of the unfolding of the lives of two of our country's greatest college teachers—these are all good pasture.

There is no imprisoning of the spirit and there is no great literature that may not be the occasioning of an "opening," of a time of devotion. I know of a man who had such an opening as he read Olive Schreiner's *Story of An African Farm,* of another for whom Shorthouse's *John Inglesant,* Dostoevsky's *The Idiot,* and Tolstoy's *Resurrection* have been the occasion of such insights. They did not come at any special times of devotion or on any schedule. But when they came, devotion was increased. It is well to learn to recognize such moments and to know enough to pause and see what they mean, to stop to assimilate them. Keyserling says that in a whole lifetime we only have a few luminous seconds of insight. When they come, let a holiday be made, a time of devotion declared, and let this seed be well planted then and there. To hurry on in order to finish the book, to take up the book again "for the purpose of scaring away one's own original thoughts," is, as Schopenhauer once remarked, a "sin against the holy spirit."

In reading devotional literature, the limitations of time and the wisdom of those who have used it most profitably agree in urging the wise use of the veto. We cannot read all. We must select. Find a few spiritual *"staples"* and feed on them until you know them. Be proud to be ignorant of vast areas of the "religious book" field. Nowhere does novelty count so little as in devotional reading. Few young people today and too few of those in my generation have ever carefully read the same book through five times or even three. A real devotional book is one that you can live with year after year and that never stales or never fails to speak to some needs in your life.

It is this kind of devotional reading linked with prayer and corporate worship that will make you able to live steadily from insights that are really yours and not be up for sale to be bought and made the conduit of each new religious sensation that comes along. Bernard of Clairvaux must have had something of this in his mind when he preached one day to his brother Cistercian preachers: "If then you are wise, you will show yourself rather as a reservoir than as a canal. For a canal spreads abroad water as it receives it, but a reservoir waits until it is filled before overflowing, and thus communicates, without loss to itself, its superabundant water." Bernard then sadly adds, "In the church at the present day, we have many canals, few reservoirs." In the world at the present time we, too, have many canals, few reservoirs. The cultivation of the devotional life would redress this balance.

BIBLIOGRAPHY

A book of this type is not assisted by the continual addition of notes referring to sources, and these have been sparingly used. Particular attention may be drawn to the usefulness of the books of three authors as a further development of the thesis of this little book. These are all readily obtainable. The remaining list contains sources for further study, with the two most suitable for a beginning marked with asterisks.

Underhill, Evelyn. *The Golden Sequence*. Dutton, New York, 1933. $2.00.

_____*Concerning the Inner Life*. Dutton, New York, 1926. $1.00.

_____*Worship*. Harper, New York, 1937. $3.00.

Hügel, Friedrich von. *Selected Letters*. Dutton, New York, 1933. $3.50.

_____*Letters to a Niece*. Dutton, New York, 1928. $2.50.

_____*Life of Prayer*. Dutton, New York, 1929. $1.00.

Sperry, Willard L. *Reality in Worship*. Macmillan, New York, 1925. $2.50.

_____

Augustine. *Confessions*. Everyman's Library, Dutton, New York, 1909. 90 cents.

Bernard of Clairvaux. *On Consideration*. Oxford, New York, 1908. $1.70.

Little Flowers of St. Francis. Everyman's Library, Dutton, New York, 1908. 90 cents.

Eckhart, Meister. *Sermons*. Translated by C. de B. Evans. J. M. Watkins, London, 1924.

Tauler, John. *Discourses on the Interior Life*. Translated by S. Winkworth. McCalla, Philadelphia, 1917. 25 cents.

_____*Theologia Germanica*. Translated by S. Winkworth. Macmillan, New York, 1893. $2.00.

Thomas à Kempis. *The Imitation of Christ*. Everyman's Library, Dutton, New York, 1928. 90 cents.

Nicholas of Cusa. *The Vision of God*. Translated by E. Gurney Salter. Dutton, New York, 1928. $2.00.

Spiritual Exercises of St. Ignatius of Loyola, The. Translated by J. Rickaby. Burns, Oates and Washbourne, London, 1915.

St. Theresa, The Life of. Translated by David Lewis. Thomas Baker, London, 1904.

Scupoli, L. *Spiritual Combat*. Longmans, New York, 1935. 50 cents.

*Francis de Sales. *Introduction to the Devout Life*. Translated by Allan Ross. The Orchard Books, Benziger, New York, 1925. $1.60.

Andrewes, Lancelot. *Devotions*. Vol. I translated by John Henry Newman; Vol. II translated by J. M. Neale, Macmillan, New York, 1920. $1.20.

Penington, Isaac. *Letters.* Friends Bookshop, 302 Arch Street, Philadelphia, Pa. 40 cents.

Fox, George. *Journal.* Everyman's Library, Dutton, New York, 1924. 90 cents.

Traherne, Thomas. *Centuries of Meditation.* Dobell, London, 1908.

Pascal, Blaise. *Thoughts.* Translated by W. F. Trotter. Everyman's Library, Dutton, New York, 1931. 90 cents.

Fénelon, Francois. *Spiritual Letters to Women.* Translated by H. L. Lear. Longmans, New York, 1931. $1.25.

*Woolman, John. *Journal.* Everyman's Library, Dutton, New York, 1911. 90 cents.

Grou, Jean. *Manual for Interior Souls.* Benziger, New York, 1932. $2.25.

Kierkegaard, Søren. *Purity of Heart.* Harper Bros.

Robinson, Forbes. *Letters to His Friends.* Longmans, New York. $1.75.

Claudel, Paul. *Letters to a Doubter.* Translated by H. L. Stuart. Boni and Liveright, New York, 1927. $2.50.

Doan, Frank Carleton. *The Eternal Spirit in the Daily Round.* Beacon Press, Boston, 1928. $2.00.

Baillie, John. *A Diary of Private Prayer.* Scribner, New York, 1936. $1.50.

Oxford Book of English Mystical Verse. Oxford, New York, 1917. $3.75.

Allen, A. V. G. *Phillips Brooks.* One volume edition. Dutton, New York, 1907. $3.50.

Cushing, H. *Life of William Osler.* Oxford, New York, 1925. $12.50.

Schweitzer, A. *Out of My Life and Thought.* Holt, New York, 1933. $2.50.

Palmer, G. H. *Life of Alice Freeman Palmer.* Houghton Mifflin, Boston, 1924. $1.08.

Whitney, Janet. *Elizabeth Fry.* Little, Brown, Boston, 1936. $3.50.

Jones, Rufus M. *Finding the Trail of Life.* Macmillan, New York, 1926. $1.00.

———————*Trail of Life in College.* Macmillan, New York, 1929. $1.75.

———————*The Trail of Life in the Middle Years.* Macmillan, New York, 1934. $2.00.

Kirkland, Winifred. *As Far As I Can See.* Scribner, New York, 1936. $2.00.

Scudder, Vida. *On Journey.* Dutton, New York, 1937. $4.00.

Brinton, Howard. *Creative Worship.* Allen and Unwin, London, 1931.

Gray, Harold. *Character Bad.* Harper, New York, 1934. $2.00.

Anker-Larsen, J. *With the Door Open.* Macmillan, New York, 1931. $1.50.

Kelly, Thomas. *A Testament of Devotion.* Harper, New York, 1941. $1.00.